THIS IS NOT THE GREATEST BOOK EVER!

By Ava Maria Ochoa and
Ava Marie Stardust

CONTENTS

"This is a love story." -Fleabag

I DON'T LIKE LONG INTRODUCTIONS

Recently, I came across clear instructions from my 10 year old self (under the pseudonym "Ava Marie Stardust") to publish "The Greatest Book Ever," a book I've started and quit writing about a dozen times with a former "friend." This book was intended to be a self-help book, because we were perfect and everyone else was gross. It covered tutorials and life hacks on hygiene, food recipes, clothes, skincare, you name it.

I don't think I can do so. Besides the fact that this ex-friend might legally own her portion of the book, I also don't think I can publish something that lives up to that title. So the book stays, forever half-finished, in a dusty corner of my room. In the words of my ex-friend, her copy was burned years ago.

I've decided to instead write a memoir dedicated to the time when I made it. All diary entries are real things I wrote and said from ages 10-12, minor details edited for clarity and privacy. I include an excerpt of my part in "The Greatest Book Ever."

I will always hold love for the people in this story. I wish the best for them.

-Ava Maria Ochoa, 2024

-Ava Marie Stardust, 2014

<u>DIARY 1</u>

September 24, 2014
Dear Diary,
Today Mr. Nowak told us because school just started, we could have a cheatsheet. One sided. But we had to do it in a limited time. I didn't get very far. But he said not to do it for homework. I didn't. I DID IT FOR FUN. And then I made him a little glitter thing that said "You're the Best, Mr. Nowak!" Now, if he lets me use the rest of the cheat sheet, I'll give him the glitter thing. If he doesn't I'll make up an excuse not to give it to him. That's all for now.

October 7, 2014
Dear c?onfused diary,
He didn't accept it.

You know what I realized? Our school has never had a dance. I think we should.

Second we have a science project and me, Lauri, and Helena are gonna do it together!

JK me and Helena quit.

My mom gave me this makeup thing. It's got EVERYTHING in it.
Only one prob. She doesn't know the quality of it.

Ohhhhh. Boy.

Oh ADULTS. They think they know everything. Guards, Take them away

{pictured: a huge Ava, a koala bodyguard, a panda bodyguard, and a trembling adult}

October 8, 2014
Dear C?onfused Diary,
11 days till my b-day!

October 9, 2014
Dear c?onfused Diary,
10 days!

In science 2day we were trying to do cool stuff with light. So we went on a field trip. Outside. A bunch of people were burning leaves with magnifying glasses. I however shined a mirror light onto a prism which created two rainbows. One was perfect. And the other. Ehhh.

{Pictured:
Rainbow 1: "I'm sorry about looking like rainbow

colored bacon. :("
Rainbow 2: "Its okay :) " }

And then someone shined a light in Isami or Celeste's eyeballs. I forget which one. Both blonds.
And in computer class we made posters for a pretend party. My party is in Washington DC to go to the zoo. To see the pandas and koalas.
WHY CAGE THIS CUTENESS?

October 14, 2014
Roses are red
Violets are blue
This poem is quick
And you are poo!

(P.S. I went to six flags for Lauri's bday party!)

October 20, 2014
Today is my b-day! Yesterday was my Birthday Party. We played sardines, Trouble (a board game), Hunter Hunted, races, pin the cherry on the ice cream cone. And as usual, savage.
Savage is when you act savage-ly at the table.
(P.S I got 100 gel pens from my epic Aunt Norma and a ipad mini from my Mom, Dad, and Grandpa.)

October 2?, 2014
Dear Confused Diary,

I'd just like to say i am not a long distance runner. So why did i join cross country? Its a mystery to me.

Ya know, I think I'm more of a walker.

OFFICIAL PRETTINESS SCALE ON THE NEXT PAGE -
>

OMG you actually fell for that? Man, you are so self-confident. And it's kind of mean to figure out how pretty I think you look! And plus, stop reading my diary: unless that's my future self. Then in that case, congrats for graduating Ada Lovelace Classical School! But if your NOT my future self, stop reading, like right now. Or else, you'll end up like this:

{pictured; coffin labeled "SNOOPY PERSON"}

I THOUGHT SO.

But, if your my future kid go tell Mommy right away that you read her old diary and then put yourself in a timeout. And congrats for learning to read.

Stay there until you feel sorry.

November 3, 2014
Today's my grandpa's birthday. He's on my mom's side of the family. Speaking of mom's side, Aunt Norma is hopefully making her signature garlic bread 4 Christmas. Hopefully. I can't wait!

(P.S. My shoes are floppy.)

November 7, 2014

Dear Confused Diary,

Yesterday. I went to Helena's house all day. Ivan (Helena's little brother) broke Helena's mason jar, which supposedly, is like, the thing. Helena says she like, knew it would happen. Do you think she can mindread? BTDUBS, she/we went shopping. I got shirts, pants, and sneakers. There were these SketchAir shoes and they were to die for. They had these things at the bottom which made you feel like you're walking on air. Talk about AWESOME! I swear the shoes were loving my feet.

I'm going to Helena's at 4:30 for a sleepover. Did you know in Helena's family, you never eat lunch on weekends. I mean imagine if you had a burger in front of you and you weren't allowed to eat it because it was in a bullet proof glass case, wouldn't you be jealous? I'm mean, come OOONNN!!!!! :) :)

November 2014,

Dear C?onfused Diary,
Today was...cool. I went to Helena's house and me, Helena, and her brother all played together. It was cray-cray.

You know, Helena's MY BFFAEAEAEAE. And i'm very protective of her.

{Pictured: a very glamorous drawing of Helena. Ava is holding her from behind.}

OK so maybe I'm clingy

But seriously, she's awesome. She's stubborn at times (like me), she's nice, and she's beautttifuuulll. And if ANYONE tries to take her away from me, GONE.

I'm like her BODYGUARD

{Pictured: another very curvaceous drawing of Helena in a movie-star dress, Ava dressed as a male body guard}

But ya know, it's really weird, cause boys never seem to notice her. And its just because she laughs and yells at them. Gosh, lighten up.

Ya know, she's got like the longest eyelashes in the school. And like the biggest eyes. But the thing is, your eyebrows are as big as your eyes. And her eyes are huge. So...ya know...yeah.

Anyway, at school, we're doing a project on a book our class read. It's called "Rules." Me and Helena are working together. We're doing a scrapbook from Kristi's point of view. We're working on it tomorrow. With Glitta! Epic BTDUBS, in a couple of minutes I'm going to gymnastics and it is a lint war going on in there. It's like all the lint in the world traveled there, had lint babies and started a ~~town state country~~ universe with it.

November ? 2014
Dear confused diary,

My day was

BLEECH!

Not :(not :) just :l

November ? 2014,
Dear C?onfused Diary,
Yesterday was Helena's b-day party. It wasn't supposed to be a sleepover, but I slept over anyway. Yeah...whatever. Well...bye...for now >:)

November ? 2014
Dear Confused Diary,
Today, Lee said he had a girlfriend and shes in 6th grade. And supposedly, they made out. He's totally lying. Who does that at 10? Plus, the boys started a club, SHA (Sherlock Holmes Agency) Lee said I could come, Oliver said I had to take the test first. Lee said I got in. Oliver said I didn't. I didn't. I'm kinda sad, but the other boys wouldn't have wanted me anyway.

Dear c?onfused Diary,
SQUEE!! They let me in. I'm an intern or an assistant or something. OMG, in music class 2day, Jesus, Lee, and Toby were playing paper football so Mr. White gave us a popquiz. And since I'm horrible at music and this is a grade, I burst into tears and sobbed. Because it wasn't even MY fault. Then Lee started

crying. He said he was faking it, but Helena said that boys don't fake tears. Also she and Cleo say Lee has a crush on me. Ohhh boy. Oh and my old 4th grade teacher, Ms. Evil, called me irritating.

Dear c?onfused Diary,

OMG! Oliver just invited me to a club of his! Plus, he said he was pissed off. Something about Lee and sports. Don't u get it? Oliver talked to me about his feelings. Like who does that? Unless...wait a second theres no WAY he likes me. Unless...ya know I gotta stop doing that. Ya know, actually Oliver AND Lee (PP)(Popular People) have been talking to me way more than they ever did. ..ever. That's kind of weird. Okay..moving on..okay.

Helena, also, during morning recess, said that Lee was pointing at me. CREEPY! I wonder what they were talking about. Ya know in projects Oliver does most of the work. Actually, in ANYTHING Oliver does most of the work. People copy off him all the time. He's a straight A student. Lee, on the other hand, does his homework at school. In the first quarter he got 2 B's like THAT. Total opposites. But opposites attract. Oliver and Lee are BFFs. And when Oliver, Jesus, and Lee played a game of truth, they all would have kissed Cleo out of all the other girls in Room 14. That PROVES im uncrushable. That means NO ONE has a crush on me. But Helena and Cleo think that Lee has a crush on me. WTH? (what the heck) Ohhhhhhh........boy.

Later thoughts

Yesterday was the Barnes and Noble Ada Lovelace Talent Show! I sang, and it. Was. EPICCC!!! I totally ROCKED IT!!! Even old GRAMMY who I didn't even know liked it. Me and Helena are applying for this awesome school...but I'm really scared. What if I don't get in but Helena does? Or the other way around? What about my friends? I'm going to totally miss them. I hope I don't BREAKDOWN. If I do, Oh boy. When I break down. My knees and fingers don't work. If I leave, here's what i think will happen.

{Pictured: Six images of Ava, slowly descending into tears. The last image Ava is a puddle of tears, and Helena is standing over Ava.}

Except a LOT more tears

Its almost Christmas!!!!
Theres some stuff I want.
I want.......

Ava's Christmas List
    1. Crayola Magic marker Maker
    2. Cute dress from Grace Anderson
    3. Softest bunny EVER from Cricket
    4. Candy (Junior Mints, Hot tamales, etc.)
    5. Catgirl Barbie Doll

December ?, 2014
OMG! I totally thought I had lost you forever! (cause I lost you) Ya know..I gotta surprise for you! Its called...(drumroll, please)
Vaca in Toledo, Ohio with my cousins. I have some BAD news too. Since my cousins (though fun and hilarious) are a teeny weensy bit nosy, I might not be able to write in you for a while. So sorry! But I will write in you whenever I can. Also I have this science thing I have 2 do, but it will get done. I hopefully promise

January ?, 2015
omg! I lost you again! Sry I didn't bring you on the trip. Okay...well, forget about that. I took a shower this morning and my hair wouldn't do anything. And I hadn't had breakfast yet so i was hungry and tired and frustrated so I burst into tears. So my dear loving mommy made me toast with butter, just how I like it. (My mom signed me up for the test) Oh! And Mockingjay (ya know the Hunger Games and Katniss and stuff) came out! :) !! But Helena saw it w/o me! And so did Cleo! Both of my top BFFs! But I'm

prob gonna see it later. Cross your fingers! SQUEEEEEEEEEEEEEEE!!!
Plus we're going out for breakfast and shopping for a Christmas tree.

Sry but there a lot of (boy) things I haven't filled you in on (such as...I'll tell you later!) But right now im totally into Catgirl gotta go. Bye!

January 17, 2015
Its Jan 17 and I got everything I wanted, including Catgirl barbie and the Crayola Magic Marker Maker. And I did a project. I took my BORING bulletin board, AND I DID a makeover!

{Pictured: Bulletin board labeled "2 awesome to show"}
It was covered in buttons, sequins, googly eyes, and fake diamonds.

I'm an expert in beauty. Inner, outer, you name it.

Do ya know that as soon as you leave your house, BOOM the government is watching you? It kinda creeps me out.

January ? , 2015
Let's talk about the future. My dentist appointment is Feb, 5, and my moms b-day is Feb 6. I have NO idea what to get her. Valentine Day is Feb. 14 the same

day I do the test to get into all the other schools. I'm so nervous! :) ! :(! Me and Helena are both doing it on Valentines Day! Also we are having a tea party! I just don't know when. I'm Ava in Wonderland and Helena is the Queen of Helenas. Also I can't wait for Easter. Got to go! Bye!

January, 2015
A lot of weird things between Oliver and Lee and me have happened :(

Lee
- After I closed my locker Lee was right behind me so I my hand accidentally touched his...(man boobs)
- I know there are a lot of things, but I just don't remember them. But they happened! What? They did!
- Oh yeah he had a dream where....ummm... lets just say we got VERY close. In his dreams! Literally.

Oliver
- Oliver talks to me about his feelings. A LOT.
- About his old crush Sarah
- About Lee
- About his LIFE
- About his NEW crush Mara.

That kind of disappointed me, though.
Because, like a LOT of other girls, ummmm...I may have a crush on Oliver. (blushing)

It started when I was Little. I told Zara, Zara told Shane, and Shane told Oliver. And I denied it. Ughhhhh...It wasn't true though. I only liked him because of his looks. And Nowwww..
(Blush)

OLIVERATHON
- He's kewt (blush)
- He likes sports
- Hes clueless
- Hes nice
- Hes honest (mostly)
- Hes... perfect
- He doesn't care what other people think of him.
- Hes cool
- He's PP
- He's a challenge

Everybody but me will disagree with this but...I think me and him are
PERFECT!

One problem. NO ONE knows that. Except for Michele and Isami. They think we're perfect. But you know what? If it ever MIGHT work out (which it won't) I'll do it. I'll take the chance. And if it doesn't I'm okay with friends. Or best friends. Mmmmmmmm. Huuuuuuu (sigh). I SO like him. He...

so...perfect.

I got a call today about the test on Feb 14th Valentines Day. You know. THE test? Seriously? Ok I'm freaking out. Let's change the subject. Let's talk about me. I am DEFINITELY not the prettiest but I'm not ugly. I'm pretty, not beautiful. But I'm getting INNER beauty. And sometimes it shows on my outer beauty. It's not weird to check yourself out. What? It's NOT! IT'S NOT!

{There are several sentences in here directly quoted from the movie Dear Dumb Diary, one of Ava's favorite book series and movies at the time.}

Goodnight!

January, 2015
Lee broke my barrette/clip. He says he'll buy me another one. He won't (probably). Its cute though. Oliver asked me about a plastic bracelet and I have no idea what hes talking about. I'll ask him about it tomorrow. Ohh..they're BOTH so cute and awesome, but Oliver still wins.

Ariana Grande is AWESOME!

{Pictured: drawing of Ariana Grande}

Wayy cuter :)

These days my drawings are really bad!

January 2015
Dear C?onfused Diary,
Today I asked Ms. Jeanine if we could listen to music. No. She said it was freetime. I asked. No. When I leave this school, I will not miss Ms. Jeanine. Or. Ms. Evil. Or. Ms. Quinn. They are NOT good with kids. I have no idea why they even became teachers. Oh and I won't miss Ms. Crawford either. She's the principal. She doesn't let me use ear muffs.

So far you (diary), Helena, Cleo, and MAYBE Mandy are my BFFs. Mostly you and Helena. Gotta go. I'll finish this later. Bye!

-Ava

January 28, 2015
In 3 days its Feb. After that ITS 14 more days till Valentines Day. And. The. Test. My mom is buying me a new comforter. Its blue with white designs on it.

I got laptop bling. Its very hard to remove.
{Pictured: laptop bling on paper}

Cool right? Ya know what else is cool? Oliver is lefthanded! Like me! I mean so is Matthew but Matthew isn't popular. It just makes me want/love him more. Gotta go. Explain l8r.

-Ava

February 2015

When I woke up something was in the air. I went downstairs. We had my favorite kind of eggs, which is scrambled, with sauteed peppers and shredded cheddar cheese. Also with buttery toast and bacon. My mom let me use her expensive paint and her ultra fancy paint paper to well, paint. I spent over an hour on my drawings, while she painted 3-4 rocks! She likes painting rocks. And she's good at it.

In the basement, she found a present Grandma Boopy gave to me when I was little! It was a clay book. And clay. The clay went bad, but Mom says I/she can get some more. And on Feb. 21st maybe that's when I can get my layered hair cut. I'm so excited. We watched the Super Bowl halftime show., I wasn't really paying attention, but the food on the table was great. We really pigged out. We got a call today saying we don't have school tomorrow. I have no idea what I'm gonna do. I'll figure that out later. Bye!

-Ava

March, 2015

No school yesterday. I went to Helena's house, did my QAR, and pigged out on candy. Also...I did the test. And ya know what? I saw a lot of my school friends there. I just didn't see that coming. My mom went to Florida. I forget why. I'll ask her when she comes back which is tomorrow. My ipad also kind of...crashed. But I know I can figure this out. Right? I know you are dying to know, Oliver checkup? Still just as cute and ya know what? He's GREAT at Pizzeria? (unlike me :))

Bad news. Turns out he's a jerk to everyone but pretty much me. But he's SO nice to me! I know every girl who has a crush wants the boy to like her back. I'm not any different. But this seems... different. Because I don't like him JUST for his looks (although he is REALLY cute!). I know how polite and nice he secretly is. And I refuse to give up on him. Oh why? LOVE?
-Ava O.

February 2015
Tiny Journal Entry
By Ava O.

You"ll notice that I'm writing in a square piece of paper. Folded twice. I know its not the highest quality journal, but its better than the one they gave us. Which is poo. Its a sparkly piece of paper of top of cut up tiny little pieces of college ruled paper and underneath is just a flimsy piece of cardboard. How its attached? A little plastic spring. That rolls RIGHT OFF. So yeah.

Also, Lee's dream/daydream came to life. He said that the girls would get the computers forever. And since the boys took advantage of the sub teacher and let themselves play before lunch even ended, the sub told Ms. Villanueva. At least, I THINK that's how you spell her name. Anyways, Ms. Villanueva was mad at the boys for taking advantage of poor whittle miss-whatever-her-name-is. So now the girls get the computer today AND tomorrow. So... yeah. Also, try to draw a person making a duckface. It's IMPOSSIBLE.

Anyway, so yeah.

It's over.

Signed,

Ava O

March 2015
Science Olympiad! I spent over 7 hours with Helena working on the board. I'm hungry

March 2015,
Ok so science olypmpiad is over. Me + Helena didn't win so thats disappointing, but whatever. I don't

have time to be jealous. Also at school I switched seats now I sit next to Lauri, Mark, and JAKE*
*I ALWAYS sit next to Jake, Samuel, or Alex.

But I can work it. Right? Tomorrow is my first day NOT sitting with Cleo. I'm sad that I won't sit with Cleo anymore :(also I'm sorry for not writing in you that much these days I will try to make a effort to write more often. Well I'm tired so I will go to bed now

April 2015
Ok guys I haven't done an entry omgod omgod We are going to have SexEd very soon (tomorrow) I'm getting my top braces in 5 days and...boy trouble! So like 4 days ago Oliver came over to me and said "I need to talk to you. Alone." I thought he was gonna admit his huge crush on me!

He instead said, "Ezra has a crush on you. He's serious. Tell no one." Ezra isn't cute, but he's super nice. I told Helena five minutes later. Bye!

P.S. I'm a vegetarian now

END OF DIARY 1

<u>DIARY 2</u>

November 10, 2015
Tuesday
Dear Diary,

Hello. You have a lot to catch up on. Okay, so Oliver left, first of all. (Yes, I know, a tragic thing), but now that i think about it, Oliver wasn't really that nice. Especially to Lee, who is my new Crush! (Don't tell anyone!). And also BTW, there is a school DANCE at the end of the year. And at the end of the year, I'm going to ask HIM to the dance. Michele has a crush on Lee (she has many crushes, over 50) which is bad. And Lee has a crush on Cleo. But Cleo likes Dennis. And Dennis likes Cleo. But luckily for me, Michele doesn't KNOW I also have a crush on Lee. Only 3 other people know this 1) Helena, whose crush is Emanuel, 2) Ramona, because she wouldn't talk to me until I told her, 3) Lauri, whose crush is… actually I forget. I'll ask her again later. But Lauri swore on her LIFE that she wouldn't tell anyone, so if she does…>:) Anyway, tomorrow is veterans day, so:
{Pictured: American flag made out of kitty cat washi tape}
Great job saving the world and stuff.

Oh, also (this is going to sound so girly) I've decided to stop having sulfates in my shampoo. And also, I'm a vegetarian right now, future Ava Marie. I've been

24

one for like, over a year.

And I am 12 now! Here is a better flag:

{Pictured: a better American flag}

Have a happy Veterans day! Talk to you tomorrow!

November 11, 2015

Wednesday! <3

Dear Diary,

Okay I have some other stuff to tell you. Lee thinks I'm the 2nd prettiest girl (which I don't think is true, because I look like poo) and I am second to Cleo. I really don't care though. Because 1) Cleo's not interested 2) I'm going to be the one to ask Lee to the dance. So HA!

<u>LATER ON</u>

Okay so, I made two drawings today (both including glitter, of course) and I had hot chocolate and an egg sandwich. Then my dad said I had to get ready and get dressed. I looked in the mirror and realized that I had REALLY long lower lashes. And at first I was like *man, these eyelashes look good,* but then I thought *Thats so conceited of me! Who cares about their EYElashes?* Thats what a lot of my self-conversations go like. Also, I'm writing a book called "The Greatest Book Ever" It's gonna be awesome. I'm still on my rough draft though. But after its done, I'm going to put it into hardover. It will blow your mind.

LATER ON…

Okay, so we just went to this pep rally, which was super boring, but afterward, at 2:00, we had lunch, which tasted awesome because I was so hungry, and dessert.

How dessert happened

{Pictured:
Lady selling food saying "would you like some dessert?"
Man selling food saying "$2 to fill up a plate"
A muslim woman wearing a hijab, labeled "Indian person, not a ninja"
Ava wearing her custom ink white shirt with a pink heart, making heart eyes at the food and the muslim woman
Ava's dad saying "Sure. Blah. Blah. Blah. Ava don't take too much." }

After dessert, a person from the deaf club came and asked us for donations. We gave $2. Okay so here is what the rally is about.

1) So some people didn't like mexico.
   {Pictured: a person saying "I have to get out"
   Another person wearing a cap and "gang" shirt saying "Yolo, swear word, swear, swear."}
2) So they escaped with their kids illegally.
       {Pictured: One person climbing over a fence, telling a second person "Come on!"}
3)   And those kids, called undocumented kids,

are not allowed many scholarships or money in general
{Pictured: A sad person holding a painting, a second person wearing sunglasses saying "Even though you won the art show, we can't give you the money"}
4) So people are changing the rules.

The End

EVEN LATER ON…
Okay so I keep hurting myself.
So first, I hurt my pointer and middle finger by banging them against a wall on accident (it scabbed). Then, I hurt my thumb at gymnastics (handstand gone wrong). Then I cut my leg shaving.

And our tumbling meet is coming up, and all you get to wear is a leotard. No pants, no shorts, no bra, no underwear, NOTHING.
#PORN (Not Really)

November 12, 2015

Thursday
Dear Diary,
Okay. its pretty awesome. My day went fine, my art class was cool (we were making Frida Kahlo shadow boxes) and its very satisfying writing a diary everyday. I need to start to get my book together. Also, Lauri's crush is Dennis + Neil. Here's how my shadow box will be like!

{Pictured: Frida Kahlo in a box with a letter, inside

the letter reads, "Oh feet, why do I need you when I have wings to fly."}

Her story is SO SAD!!!!
(Search it up)

DIY Lip Balm
You will need...
1) Vaseline
2) old candle or 2 crayons or beeswax
3) Eyeshadow (for color)

1) Put together in bowl
2) Heat up
3) Put in Container

November 15, 2015
SUNDAY!
(Yes I know I skipped, but I forgot about this on the other days)

Dear Diary,
Okay, on Friday...I spent the day at Helena's house, since my parents couldn't take care of me. Also I've discovered 3 things, (which include Lee)
1) Michele has Lee's #! She can text him whenever he wants. But Lee has the type of Phone that only certain brands of phones can call.
2) Lee's dad is sick/ got hurt. Apparently its bad. He said its uncomfortable to talk about it. And yet, he still told me it! :) ! Aww!
3) His sister is REALLY good at gymnastics. I'm

talking front handsprings, back handsprings, you name it.

Me, I'm only insanely flexible. That's an understatement.

Unfortunately, even though I'm flexible, I can't do that crazy stuff. But hey, most people can't do what I do. So that's something to be proud of.

November 16, 2015
MONDAY!
Dear Diary,
False alarm. Lauri only has a crush on Neil. Also B +B (by the by) I have a salt lamp now. It helps with my spastic bronculosis. And the other remnants of diseases I have/had.

POP QUIZ!
Mwahahaha! You think you could get away with reading MY diary without getting a quiz? HA!
Tally up your points!
1) Your siblings destroy the project you've been working on for weeks. You...
    a) Cry (1)
    b) Scream at them (3)
    c) Chirp happily and begin again (-2)
    d) Get frustrated, then move on (2)
    e) Do nothing. YOu don't have siblings (4)
    f) Scream **** (-6)
2) You trip over someone's foot, and your art supplies go everywhere. You...

a)   Pick them up quietly, planning your revenge (-2)
b) Sob until your out of tears (1)
c) Chirp, pick them up happily and skip away (-3)
d) Do nothing. You're homeschooled. (4)
e) Scream **** (-6)
3) You run out of duct tape. You...
   a) Nag your parents to get you more until you win (-1)
   b) Say Eh and shrug, then use your parents (3)
   c) Do something else (2)
   d) Scream **** ! (-6)
   e) Cry (1)

(-9)-(3)= your a psychopath/ you have no life. NEVER say those words!
4-12= your fine, I guess
13-15= your cool, you can hang out with ME!
16-18= your a bae. Also known as Ava Marie Stardust.

November 17, 2015
TUESDAY!!
Dear Diary,
Okay, some more gossip. I'm pretty sure Isami has a crush on Samir, and Samir has a crush on Isami. Also, Ella has a crush on Lee. All this competition! Also Caroline made Michele promise that if Caroline asked out Reilly to the dance, Michele would ask out

Lee! This is terrible!! UGHH!

Also, I thought the Latin test was on <u>Thursday</u> but it was TODAY! But, I have some good news: Lauri took me home today and took me bowling, instead of JUST having me stay home alone for a long time. It was actually really fun. But Lauri's mom swears a lot. At least she doesn't smoke. Anyway, tomorrow is Wednesday, but we don't have any school because its report card pick up day (Straight A's, people) and I'm going over to Helena's house. Yay!

November 18 2015
Wednesday! <3
Dear Diary,
As you should have known from your previous entry, I had no school yesterday.
I did several things at Helena's house.
1) Make a pink perler bead heart.
2) Go to several stores, including Marshalls where I got this key:
{Pictured: Ava's Key, labeled "Key to the Heart" and Helena's key, labelled "Friendship Key: They Key to Everything}

Afterwards, I went to gymnastics, had some dinner (and a stolen samosa) and now here I am. Also, I put the key on a string and turned it into a necklace! Also, Mom said I couldn't have a new coat, and I had to use an old hand-me-down that my cousin had. The insulation is poo, and it isn't FUZZY!

ARGHHH!

November 19 2015
Thursday=nothin

November 20, 2015
Friday=who cares

November 21 2015
Saturday= sleepover with Helena+ made nutella eos!

November 22, 2015
SUNDAY!
Dear Diary,
DID MY PERFORMANCE AT THE TALENT SHOW/ FUNDRAISER! I was in a beautiful dress and I sang "Skyfall" and "Last Christmas."

And then I bought a sketchbook. When I got home, I was floppy and took a nap with Mommy :p sleeping beside me. Then I finally drank some of my new *Sleepytime Tea.* Then I had some CHEESE ENCHILADAS!
So now I'm okay. Bye!

November 23, 2015

Monday 8 (8 is the new "!")

Upcoming events=
Gymnastics Tournament: next tuesday
Spelling bee: somewhere next week

TODAY:
Okay. It's official. Lauri hates Cleo.
Even though its three months late, Lauri is having a birthday party, AND DO YOU KNOW WHO'S INVITED?

NOT Cleo, Thats Who!
(And I'm pretty sure neither is Helena)
(But I forget)

Here's who IS INVITED!
ME! JULIE! Mandy! And of course...LAURI!

And last, but CERTAINLY NOT Least...
I want/think I'm gonna get a BOB!
Anyway...BYE!

November 24, 2015
TUESDAY!
Dear Diary,
Ohmyogdmystomachhurts. Okay now its betterish. Anyway me + Helena are doing nonsecret SecretSanta. To each other. So you want to know what I'm getting her?
  1) A cool wooden bristle tek brush
  2) A vintage Coke poster
  3) Coke

4) Aladdin
5) uhh...IDK. But something else.
   OH yeah! Hair stuff!

   Anyway...
   BYE! So, yeah!

November 25, 2015
WEDNESDAY
Anyway I forgot to tell you this but Michele has her period. And she massages her boobs to make them bigger. And she masterbades. Also Caroline recently got her period which she tried to keep a secret from me and totally failed. Also I think Ramona read my diary. I think she's been going through my stuff lately. I'm gonna ask her to stop

November 26, 2015
Thursday= nothing happened

November 27, 2015
FRIDAY
Dear Diary,
I told Helena about the Lauri party. Helena wanted me to tell Cleo, so I did. Helena and Cleo surprised me though. They actually hated her too. So then I told Cleo the truth about Lauri hating her. I never should have told them. Now I feel terrible. Now Helena thinks Lauri's ignoring her and being a bully.

But actually, she's got it all twisted up. Lauri's not IGNORING HER, they're just not really close friends. So now Helena doesn't want me to talk to Lauri. But I have a childhood instinct to do whatever Lauri wants. And I fear her. Whatever. In other news, here is me and Helena's crush chart:

Who we wish liked us:
Helena: Emanuel
Me: Lee

Who likes us:
Helena: Shane
Me: Mark

:(:(:(:(

Also my mom's work friend made me more cool paper stuff, this time:
TEAR OUT PAD NOTEBOOKS!
One for me, one for Mommy

November 28, 2015
Sat: brunch, dance class

November 28, 2015
SUNDAY <3
Today was...fine, I guess.
Nothing really happened.
Nothing...at all really.

November 30, 2015
Monday: nothing

December 1, 2015
Tuesday: minifight with Helena but whatever.
Plus a gymnastics tournament where I WAS FABULOUS!
But I didn't have time to receive my prize, so I'm gonna collect my prize tomorrow. But Jessie scored #1 in her heat, and Scarlet scored #2 in her heat. But this is my first time, so I probably scored 20th place.

December 2, 2015
WEDNESDAY!
Omg omg okay so today I had a science test today but I couldn't study that much because I had my competition and I couldn't complete my math h.w. But I got sympathy from both teachers which is awesome anyway yeah it was cool. Also Helena asked for a DIARY TO WRITE HER FEELINGS IN, which I take as a good sign. But anyway on my way home after the bus in my mom's car, we stopped by the park to get my prize and I got
5th Place!
OMG!
{Pictured: ribbon labeled "5th Place Hamilton Park Gymnastics Team"}
And our park won 1st place for Advanced Beginner!

Which is the level I'M in! Yay! We got a trophy and everything! Omgomgomgomgomgomgomg

{Pictured: Trophy with gymnast on top}
Okay anyway bye!

December 3, 2015
Thursday: Helena said the initials "B.S." and minifight

December 4, 2015
Friday: fights over.

December 5, 2015
SATURDAY!
Dear Diary,
Today was cool. I went out to this new restaurant for brunch, went to dance class, organized my room, went to a restaurant with Helena, and now we are having a sleepover at my house. I just gave her a diary to write in, so here's what we look like:

{Pictured: two girls, writing in separate diaries}

She called or is calling her diary "Helen," which is her Latin name. (mine is Aurora) should I name you Aurora? I'll ask Helena!

I asked.

So from now on, I'll call you Aurora/ Diary. Aurora

is new, fresh, and beautiful, while Diary is a classic, go-to name. Also, right after we came home from dinner, me and Helena decorated cookies and got drunk on sugar. We recorded it. We are so DUMB. But you know what? That's okay. And you know what else? I was reading my old diary, and I am so DUMB. By the way, here are some things you should know about me

NAME: Ava Marie Stardust
BIRTHDAY: 10-20-2003
MOM: Bridget Ochoa
DAD: Elijah Ochoa
BFFAEAE: Helena Kari Pruitt
BFF: Cleo/ Ramona
BUS FRIEND: Lauri
FAV MOVIE: Cinderella/ Alice in Wonderland
BFFAEAE B-DAY: 9-10-2003
CRUSH: YOU SHOULD ALREADY KNOW BY NOW
FAV SPORT: Gymnastics

Also at the sleepover we did this makeup thing where you try to make the other person look as different as possible. I ended up giving Helena a makeup bruise (on accident) and Helena gave me two giant black moles (on purpose.) Also to wash off the makeup, we made a cinnamon, honey, and baby oil mask. Also while we were watching Rudolph the red nosed reindeer we had sleepytime tea, which reminded Helena of her childhood.

December 6, 2015
SUNDAY!
Dear Diary,
Okay
1) I organized my room
2) We went to the botanical garden
3) We went out to lunch
4) I'M SO EXCITED FOR SECRET SANTA! I can't wait for Helena to open her presents.
5) Bye! <3 u guys!

December 7, 2015
Monday:
Okay, so today I tried to make breakfast, but it ended up looking like a squishy lump. Which it was.
And Helena hugged me today too, which does not happen as often.

December 8, 2015
Tuesday
Okay so tomorrow I'm going to pack presents (for Helena) and tomorrow is our snowflake serenade, and if you're wondering what that is, it's where your parents come to see you cramped, standing on a stage with 59 other kids with B.O. who are singing (offkey) a mix of Christmas carols, Latin Hanukkah songs, and old folklore songs. Also Lauri's Christmas party is on Sunday.

Also I have some bad news. Yesterday, when I went to the doctor's office to get a cancer treatment shot, the subject got to W. Now diary, W is a very hard subject to talk about for me. W is humiliating and painful. I'll tell you my story.

W appeared. They tried the common way of treating it, which didn't work, and just left me screaming, crying, in pain and limping. 97 months of that). So they tried their uncommon trick, which almost always left me in pain, even more pain than before. (2 months). Oh my gosh I'm now crying while writing this because I'm remembering the pain. Then they honestly had no idea what to do because the W weren't going away. So they tried using chemicals that weren't tested for W. I could tell the doctors were getting nervous, and me and my parents were getting frustrated because we were giving them all this money to bring me in pain. But luckily, it worked. Or so I thought. A few weeks after the W were gone, large ugly, giant, disgusting bumps took their place. I was so self-conscious. And when I wasn't, someone would ask me about the bumps (which were even worse than the W in the first place) and I would get self conscious again. It was awful! It IS awful. Anyway, the doctor said that I might have another W, which brought back the memories, which made me cry. I swear, tears are streaming down my face right now.
Anyway, Bye.

December 11, 2015
FRIDAY!
OMG! I got a ton of cool presents from Helena. But I forgot to bring them home. ARGHH! Also, Ramona got me a nice pad of paper and colored pencils, but she kept on crying and lying the whole day.

December, 2015
Winter Break
I got a ton of presents! I got hair stuff, movies, silly putty, $40, magazines, Alice in Wonderland miniature tea set, Alice in Wonderland Charms, leg-warmers, gum, and a cardboard house.
{Pictured: elaborate cardboard house}

January 1, 2016
NEW YEARS! 2016! 2016!
Yay! To start off the new year, I'm doing a deep cleaning of my sections of the house. Its going great so far. And so, dear diary, happy new year.

January 10, 2016
Dear Diary,
A lot of things have happened. Helena ignored me for an hour, which is annoying, and Michele wrote this book for Young Authors.
This is an excerpt.

"M<u>amona</u> is annoying."
"M<u>aroline</u>" is a jerk."
"M<u>alena</u> is a know-it-all."
"Fl<u>ava</u> is airheaded and dumb."
She said it wasn't based off of anybody she knows, so...
LIAR!

Also, Ramona said that Caroline didn't like me. So either Caroline doesn't like me, or, as usual, Ramona is lying. And so, for MY young authors, I'm going to write a book that I was already gonna write about, but never got to it. Also Michele likes Toby, and LOVES Dennis. And now, Lauri HATES Neil.
But Helena <u>did</u> get my laptop for me, and shared part of her orange with me.

{Pictured: A very beautiful Helena wearing a dress, heels, and holding an orange, labeled "she would never wear this"}
{In tiny writing: "But I wish she wouldn't ignore me or not tell me things. }

AND my mom (as usual) was SUPERNICE and
1) Put away my clothes and organized my leg-warmers
2) Got Daddy to do MY chore
3) AND let me try out my beauty stuff
4) Also, my mom gave me a french braid!
   Thank you Mommy!
   Goodnight!

January 11, 2016

Ramona is insane. She's planning on "overthrowing" the popular group, which BTW, is super nice. They let me join in on their "Bean-boozle" challenge. Kayley and Cleo are the nice, funny girls of the group. Dennis and Toby are the nice funny guys of the group. Also being "popular" is overrated, Also Nora just wants to kill everybody. You know what, I'm gonna draw pictures of my friends. Because I feel like it.

{Pictured: Two tiers. The top tier has full length drawings of Helena, Cleo, Michele, Caroline, and Ramona. On a lower tier, a cat, a fat small Ava, and a dog, are shown together.}

Anyways Diary, why do I have such pretty friends? That's a question for later. Bye!

Continued January 11, 2016

Dear Diary,

I forgot to tell you that yesterday, Helena sent me a long, heartfelt message. She said so many wonderful things, and showed off her new trivia knowledge. (Speaking of trivia, Michele won the school trivia-athon! I was first runner-up, and really wanted to give the school trivia-thon a go, but I was still really happy/proud of Michele. So now, Michele has won the school trivia-thon twice!)

It's times like this that make me appreciate Helena. Also, I asked Helena if she would share her salad with me. She said, straight off the bat, "No." But then I told her that if she didn't, and I wrote that in my diary, then later on when I'm older and I re-read it, then I will think that Helena was mean to not share with me, even after I offered her Polish Milk Chocolate. After a moment, she looked away thoughtfully, then started filling salad onto my paper napkin. I expected only a leaf or two of her salad, but she gave me all the types of leaves, tomatoes, the dressing, and then some vegetable she tricked me into eating because she knew I wouldn't like it. But we laughed about it.

And Helena confirmed that Caroline doesn't like me. That's okay. Also, I had a terrible headache today. It was horrible. But neither of my parents could pick me up, so I had to wait it out. Also, since Sunday, I left this oil in my hair to make it soft after I washed it out. I washed it out today, which is Tuesday. Its ultra-soft and thick. Its so nice to touch. Like...like a new blanket. Anyway, its getting late and I need sleep.

Goodnight Diary!

(P.S. Your full name is Amatia Diary Ochoa, but I call you Diary for short)

A.D.O. —>thats you

January 12, 2016
Wednesday

Dear Diary,
I am writing with my right hand. Why? Gymnastics! Here's how:

What was supposed to happen:
{Pictured a handstand on the beam, then a dismount on the beam}

But I fell off the beam backwards and hit my head/face and hands. My left wrist feels really messed up. Without my dominant hand, it's really hard to do stuff. So my dad wrapped it. Hope I feel better tomorrow. Bye!
P.S. I have a scratch on my head now

January 13, 2016
Dear Diary,
My hand still feels sore, but thats okay. I still wished I could have stayed home from school today though. A lot of people were concerned about my hand, but most teachers didn't notice. My scratch on my head pretty much disappeared. Also, my book for Young Authors is going to be amazing! I'm even going to get it turned into a hard copy. And my friends will be in it! It will be so cool! Helena's gonna help and stuff and if she contributes enough to the book that I already don't have, then her name will be put on the cover next to mine, and we'll both be on the cover! Its called "The Greatest Book Ever!" By Ava Marie Stardust and Helena Pruitt.

{Pictured: a book titled "The Greatest Book Ever!" on the bottom of the cover, a picture is taped picturing two girls. }

Also, Helena reminded me of something she said earlier:
"What if the whole universe is a body, and we're all just cells on it?"

Also, you know what I noticed? Michele always has perfect hair! Even her ponytails are perfect! Me? Not so much. I can barely make it through a day without my hair becoming a mess! Anyway, goodnight!
Mwah!

January 14, 2016
Dear Diary,
My wrist is doing better, and my head completely healed! Helena wouldn't share her orange with me today though. And now it's double confirmed that Caroline does not like me. Also, I think me, Helena, and Michelle made Caroline feel bad today. You see, Michelle, Helena, and I all went to a private school (which was the BEST!) and Caroline skipped daycare and preschool and went straight to kindergarten.

So while me, Helena, and Michelle were gabbing on & on about how great private school is, Caroline was just sitting there looking uncomfortable. At one point I thought she was going to cry. She moved away, saying that she "needed to get her work done." Of course soon afterwards we all felt bad about it, and invited her to come back. She did, although reluctantly, and started to relax again.

Also, Mom left today to visit her sister and dad to have a "daughter father weekend." So me and dad were left in charge of not making the house a mess. She left me a note before she left, starting with "Dear Babycakes." Babycakes is just something she calls me. Also, I forgot to tell you this, but my dad had this surgery done to his foot to remove something, so he had to wear a cloth shoe for a while, but at the doctors when they gave it a check-up, they saw that it got infected. So now Daddy has to wear the shoe for even longer.

Also, I forgot to tell you another thing. A while ago, Ramona got some dandruff shampoo in her eye, and this is what happened:

Before
{pictured: normal eye}
After
{Pictured: eye with redness and a stye}
Now
{Pictured: eye with a stye}

But, the funny thing is, I was the one who had recommended the shampoo to her! Also, Ramona and Lauri DEFINITELY hate each other. But Ramona is trying this new thing where she tries to be nice. This is working out so far, although I don't know if she's capable of being nice for long periods of time. But if she puts her mind to it, then I believe in her!

January 15, 2016

This diary is coming to an end. It's sad. But anyway about today. Me and dad went to dance class, me with a hair mask on. After that we went to a pastry shop. I got a lemon square and Daddy got an apple cake. Then we went to a meat-filled restaurant, but since I'm a vegetarian (Lauri STILL doesn't believe me) I had a cheese pizza with tomatoes. After we got home, I ate my lemon square. It was really good. Then me and Helena FaceTimed (or ft, as we abbreviate it) and did our miniature book report for class (with her doing most of the work). Then we had (me + dad) had potato tacos for dinner, and if you're wondering what potato tacos are, the science of it is pretty simple: mashed potatoes + cheese + ketchup + tortilla = potato taco. Then daddy tried his apple cake. He didn't like it. Anyway, I'm going to wash out the hair mask tomorrow, and work on my Selectiveprep, which is prep material for the test. Also tomorrow, I take my Classical School Exam, to see if I get into any classical schools. My life feels pretty good right now. I've got Helena, my best friend forever and ever and ever (BFFAEAE), Ivan, her adorable little brother, my gymnastics team, which includes my BFFSB (best friend forever since birth) Jessie, my mom and dad are really nice, I'm feeling nice, my room looks organized, and everything is great, Amatia Diary Ochoa. Including you. Goodbye.

Love <3,

Ava Marie Stardust A.M.S.

Ava Marie Stardust {Pictured: many cursive variations}

END OF DIARY 2

<u>DIARY 3</u>

January 15, 2016
Dear Diary,
You are my third diary. I am Ava Marie Stardust, in sixth grade, at Ada Lovelace Classical School. You can get more information from my second diary. If you are reading this right now let me tell you right now that I have the power of magic. If you are a kind person who reads this diary, call this number: 773-555-5555 or 773-555-5555- or even 773-555-5555. I will bless you with all my heart and may luck be with you always. But, if you read past this very page, and/or are too lazy to return this diary, then I will curse you for bad fortune to follow you for the rest of your life.
Signed,
Ava Marie Stardust
      A. M. S. Ava Marie Stardust

January 16, 2016
SUNDAY
Dear Diary,
Today was a pretty good day. I woke up, took a shower, and skipped breakfast. After a while, me and my dad went to Superdawg, where I had a grilled cheese, french fries, a pickle (which I didn't eat), and a chocolate milkshake (which I drank ALL of). After that, we went grocery shopping. We went home, and

I baked vanilla cupcakes, which didn't turn out to be a complete disaster, which is really strange, now that I think about it. But my cupcakes *did* taste a bit like corn. Well, whatever, the big point is that it didn't become a disaster.

About Helena's day. She took the classical selective enrollment test today (I'm going to be taking the test next Saturday). The test is to see if you qualified to be accepted into any classical schools. Afterwards, she watched a murder mystery show which is actually a true story. I wonder when Mom's coming home. I miss her. But I hope she's having a good time. She deserves it. But Dad's being a big help, too. Today he tried to fix the sink. Right now I hear Dad trying to force the leak to stop. I don't think it's working. Anyway, it's getting late, and I need to be awake for the work I'm going to do tomorrow. Bye!

January 19, 2016
Dear Diary,
Today was a mediocre day. More like a gloomy day. The day wasn't that good, because me & Lauri got into a mini fight. I think we had a silent truce at the end of the day/ bus ride. Anyway, my hair is greasy, so I put a LOT of eco-friendly dry-shampoo in my hair. It made my hair not greasy, but it also tangled my hair, so now it's up in a bun.
Also, my dad is/was shocked when I told him I was 90 pounds. I'm not fat! Am I?

Anyway, I don't care. Let's talk about something else: Helena. Helena has kind of stopped hugging me, which annoys me. And I'm not allowed to drink out of her water bottle, but its okay that she drinks from someone else's? Whatever.

So today Mr. Nowak told us we will not be having a cheat-sheet for our Unit 2 Science Test? What is he thinking? I'm definitely gonna flunk. But I can at least try, right? Right? Oh and I forgot to tell you that me and Helena officially qualified for the next round in the art competition! And also, we have a math test tomorrow, so I am gonna practice with Ms. Villanueva at lunch time. Anyway, it's late. Goodnight!

January 20, 2016

Dear Diary,

Today, in the morning apparently Michele and Samir got into a fight and started swearing at each other. And also, I give Helena my girl magazines after I'm done with them, so she reads them on the bus home. But one time, Samir saw Demi Lavato in one of the magazines, and said she was hot, so now Samir asks Helena everyday if she has any more "girl magazines." In social studies, Helena got my laptop for me.

And in gym, we were just talking, and Ramona asked us who we thought the Leader was. Ramona and Helena both said themselves, but Helena changed her mind to Michele. I said Michele in the beginning. Caroline said there was no leader of the group, but if there was, Michele. Michele also picked herself. Ramona was very upset about this, and she tried to strangle Michele. In gym. In the middle of a dodgeball game. Wow. Pressure's on now. At lunch I worked with Ms. Villanueva to figure out what to do for the test.

And also, Helena said that the point of this test is to beat everyone else (true) so you shouldn't help other people study. (She was talking about the selective Enrollment Test.) She said this because I said I was going to study at Ella's house on friday to study for the test. And my mom just emailed Helena's mom if Helena and her mom could come over on Sunday, also to study and for the moms to drink wine. But Helena seems really edgy lately. She and her mom are really serious about studying. But you know what I need to work on? Being able to do math problems fast. And multiplying double digit numbers in my head. Definitely. Anyway, its getting kind of late, so I'm going to sleep now.

January 21, 2016
Dear Diary,
Today was a mix of good and "meh." The "meh" part was that Helena ignored me a lot, and she got mad at me over the STUPIDEST thing(s). But the GOOD part was that I was really good in both art classes, and also, my voice sounded really good in my voice lessons. Helena took my second diary, to get ideas for HER diary (supposedly). But I swear

if she changes/copies/saves/does ANYTHING to it, I will STRANGLE HER! I'm not joking. And she better not show anybody else. But I get to see her diary too. I wonder what she writes in it. She said she didn't write much about me. I wish she would give me more hugs. I now have to <u>make</u> her give me hugs. But, for Christmas, she gave me some "IOU's", one of them saying "Free." So, I can use the "Free" one to make her make me a whole BUNCH of IOU's that all say "Hug NOW." I am an evil genius! MWA HA HA!

{Pictured: Ava as an evil genius}
Anyway, I'm still nervous about letting Helena keep my diary, but I have faith in her. After all...she returns it tomorrow

January 23, 2016
Dear Diary,
She returned it safe and sound. Also today's Saturday, because I forgot to write on Friday. But on Friday, I got picked up by Ella's mom. She made us a bunch of yummy snacks, and then we studied Selectiveprep, and took a break for Nintendo Wii, then finished studying and went to a rib place restaurant, which I didn't like. Today, I took the Classical test, and afterwards I was really tuckered out, but my dad took me to this good Mexican place, where I had a large horchata and nachos.
        Then I put on a hair mask and read part of this

organizing book called "Spark Joy" by Marie Kondo. After that, I organized my closet and took a shower, and my mom blow dried my hair and styled it pretty like hers. Then we went to ANOTHER restaurant, and when we got home, my mom put my hair into two french braids. Then we put away my laundry together, and now I'm in bed. Also, at the second restaurant, I asked my mom "If you could go back in time when you were ages 15-25, what would you tell yourself?" She said she would go back to when she was 18 to break up with her current boyfriend. When I questioned about that, she said she would tell me later. What's your answer, Diary? Tell me later!

_____

_____

Anyway, Goodnight!

{Pictured: crescent moon with a night cap and smiley face}

January 24, 2016
SUNDAY:
Became extremely sick, temperature 99.9, threw up 8 times, and because of the throwing up I lost over 3 pounds.

January 25, 2016
MONDAY:
My mom reluctantly let me stay home from school, but I still have a headache though. I'm really tired

January 26, 2016

Dear Diary,

So today Lee came to school and then left. In the middle of it. BTDUBS, I don't have a crush on him anymore. In case you didn't get that.

Also what was REALLY funny today was this: I was playing with a rubber band, when it fell into Helena's apples. I gasped, but Helena said, "Ah, I wasn't going to eat those anyway. They make me fart." (She meant to say throw up).

Anyway, me and Helena practically <u>died</u> laughing. But Helena keeps on calling me fat, dumb, and stupid, which I know are jokes, and sometimes even I call her those things, too, but I think our clique "pretend-sarcastic-bullying" is getting out of hand. And when I say "clique," I'm expanding upon just me + Helena. I'm talking about Caroline, Michele, and Ramona. Also, I've heard that Room 16 swears a lot too, including Lauri. Where has this world come to?

I hate that the point of life is to work, and I think that that is NOT right, under any circumstances. I wish I could change it. But not just a little. A lot. I would change it a LOT. Sometimes I feel as though I'm stuck, just trying to get out.

Even Helena goes with some of the stereotypes of adults, though I know she doesn't mean to. She's a good friend. I'll probably read this entry later and think, "what was I THINKING?" But that's how it goes. You gotta write in the spur of the moment. I'm a complete ALIEN.

But at least I have three friends. You/diary, me, and Helena. Anyway, its to go to sleep. I'll TTYL. Goodnight!

January 27, 2016
Dear Diary,
For some reason I was really happy this afternoon. I don't know why. But I had a really good dinner. Cheese enchiladas! And GINGER ALE! Yummies! Also, I washed my hair upstairs with my mom's shampoo and conditioner and now my hair feels super soft! Also Helena and I were talking and we decided that one day, she will take me out to Bubba Gump where we will have coconut shrimp. And I know that coconut shrimp is seafood, and I hate seafood, but I'm willing to give it a chance. I mean, Helena sure seems to like it.

Also, I know its against my vegetarianism, but maybe I won't be a vegetarian by then. So there! Also, I can choose to eat whatever I want.! Its not like if I eat meat, I die, or that I'm bound to the sacred oath of vegetarians, right? Anyway, its been a long day, so goodnight!

P.S. Tomorrow, Helena's bringing me some of her lavender tea in exchange for my Deliciosa pina colada tea!

Yay!
{Pictured: Helena and Ava, holding hands and

exchanging tea.}

Dear Diary,
January 28, 2016
Helena got mad at me because she took/snatched away a paper that *I* own, and then I snatched/took it right back. Dumb, right? And I got a 68% on a grammar test. And 100% on my math test. Also, I think Ramona has been reading in my diary. So I am going to set up some trap: hide this diary, and leave an old, fake, lying one around. Or not. I don't know. I'm lazy.
Anyway, bye.
Goodnight!

January 29, 2016
Dear Diary,
Michele is really insecure and hates Cleo because everyone "like-likes" Cleo including Toby, who Michele likes. <u>And</u> she read my diary. I think my first and/or second one.

I put in a coconut oil mask in my hair to make it soft, and I'll wash it out later for when Helena comes, which is tonight for studying for selective prep. But I hope we get to do more than just study. Yayzees!

February 2, 2016

Okay, On Sunday Helena and her mom came (but not her dad, because he's on a diet) and we studied. But after a while we got bored, so we tried to make slime, which turned in a goopy mess. It was awful. Also, me and a bunch of other people are doing "Secret Cupid" for Valentine's day, which is basically like Secret Santa.

Here's who I know:
Odette: Mark
Helena: Odette
Me: Helena
Zara: Me
Caroline: Celeste
Michele: Lee
Lee: Ariana
Ramona: Ramona
Dennis: Toby
Toby: Dennis

I only told Caroline who I got, so she better not tell. Side note in other class: Samir called Lauri a really bad word. So bad, I can't even write it.
So back to the slime, two things:
1) One day, I am going to go to Helena's house and waste HER stuff and
2) She made me glitter slime.

Here is how how to make glitter slime:

<u>Ingredients</u>
- Bowl
- Liquid glue
- Liquid glitter glue
- TIDE laundry detergent (<u>only</u> Tide)

<u>Instructions</u>
1) Mix together in bowl
2) Use until slimy!

Anyway, side note thats sad(der) I had a spastic bronculosis attack today. It was scary. Ambulance and police came, and I got <u>so</u> scared. Anyway, it was over by the time they got there, so okay...

But anyway, I was really scared. The air quality in Chicago stinks, and the exhaust at the back of the bus is terrible. All the teachers and principal and vice principal were freaked out when I got to school. But anyway, better news. My dad was on T.V. today, fighting for whatever good cause he's a part of. But apparently what he did was really important, so yay! Go him! (He's part of the Earhart Teachers Union, or ETU).

Ms. Dull said to Ramona (who is doing the ETU for her history fair project) that she/ Ramona should interview my dad. Anyway, its getting late. Bye!
Goodnight!

February 3, 2016

Dear Diary,
I don't really know what to write about. There's a lot of stuff going on.

I got rubber bands on my braces, I did terribly on my math quiz, Helena hurt her elbow, Michele hurt her legs, Michele chose Toby over Helena (ouch), all my predictions with Lauri are coming true, Helena's slime that she made especially for me went bad in one day, and way more.

I mean, I wish time would stop for a week so I could get everything done, and then resume time.

Instead I have to rush, and be/feel stressed all the time.

Also I need to bring Helena a swimming suit tomorrow. Anyway, I'm glad you're my friend. Diary. You get me. I'm too exhausted to do/write anything else, so I guess this is goodbye. For now. Till morrow! Goodnight!

P.S. For mothers day, I'm drawing her an ocean scene, and if I have time, making her a earbud holder.

February 6 or 7, 2016
Dear Diary,
Sorry I haven't been writing these days. I was busy with my mom, because although yesterday was her b-day, and she spent it with her friends, today is the family party/superbowl pig-out-and-eat-as-much-food-as-you-can day. So yeah! While Mom was hanging out with friends yesterday, I was at Jessie's

house, where I was supposed to have a sleepover, but I bailed and spent the night at my house.

I guess now I'm awkward at sleepovers unless it's with Helena. But Helena is too focused on the test to have playdates, or sleepovers, or have the chance to get sick. And I know she probably doesn't mean to, she's becoming overbearing about the test. (Helena if you are reading this right now, I'm not trying to offend you.) But I'm sure things will change once the test is over.

I dont know. I'm wierd right now. Wierd or weird?

Anyway,

Goodnight!

P.S. You are fabulous

February 8 or 9, 2016

Dear Diary,

Soon, I will literally force Helena to share her food, because I give her my stuff, when I have to COAX her to give me her stuff. Anyway, she said that she wrote five pages in her diary devoted to why she was mad at me. Also, at school, we were doing Secret Cupid, and I got Helena and told Caroline? I deliberately told her not to tell Helena. But guess what? She told Helena! And so guess what? You know how at the end of each year, I have a party, and i invite my friends? HERE'S WHO I'M INVITING:

My original plan:

Me, Helena, Cleo, Ramona, Michele

Later on:
Me, Helena, Michele, Caroline (maybe Ramona or Cleo)

Now:
Me, Michele, Cleo (maybe Ramona)

I mean, honestly Caroline! Right when I was about to trust you! And Helena said that they talk about everybody on the bus. And their secrets. Including mine. I asked Helena what she told about me, but she avoided the question. It's not that I'm mad that they talked about me, I'm mad that they won't tell me what that was! I want honesty.

Helena, when you read this, I want you to be honest. What are the three biggest secrets you've spilled about me on the bus? Go ahead. Take the pen or pencil out of the holder on the right, and fill out the sheet on the next page. If you are not dead honest, or if you write that you don't know/remember, I WILL be mad. So go ahead. Write on.

{Pictured on the next page: three empty lines, signed by Helena in print and in signature}

Anyway, she also wouldn't say "I love you" over Facetime, or any time. Does she not love me?
Do YOU not love me, Helena?

{Pictured: two checkboxes labeled Y and N, neither of which are marked. Helena's pencil marks smack in between the two choices. Underneath the Y, it says "If you checked this, write you 'I love you' here" }

Thanks for filling it out. If you've filled everything out correctly, you're a true friend. Anyway, Goodnight!

February 10, 2016
Dear Diary,
We had two quizzes today, and I think I did really well. Maybe 100%? I don't know. Anyway, after the Selective Prep test, I'm invited to a birthday party (followed by a sleepover) hosted by Sydney. I think she'll like my present, which is a bunch of beauty products!

And on the Monday after that (which is no school, because of President's Day) I'll be going to Helena's house! It's been too long! Anyways, sad news, Jessie's grandfather, or Raymond's dad, has had cancer for a while now, and today he died. I feel awful. Right now, I'm going to say a prayer. Okay, done.

Then my mom started talking about HER mom (or my grandmother) who died of lung cancer because of cigarettes. She had ignored the cancer for too long, and by the time she got it checked out, the cancer had spread through her whole body. It was too late. She died not meeting my older cousin, and not even close to meeting my dad or me. But she got a tiny chance to see Leo (another cousin) right before she died. And I told my mom how distraught I would be if I ever lost one of them (my parents.)

After that, we talked a bit longer, and now I'm getting ready (or am ready) to go to sleep

February 11, 2016
Dear Diary,
Nothing much happened today. I read Helena's diary and in some entries she called me annoying (sometimes true) and sweet (always true). Also, I saved myself time and money by making a shirt foldy thing. Its so cool.
{Pictured: shirt folder made out of cardboard and duct tape}

On Monday, I'm gonna bring it over to Helena's house to fold, fold fold! It's a miracle.
Also, Michele started shunning us (me, Helena, Caroline, Ramona) for the popular crowd. We were mad, so we set up a fake court. It ended up with all of us promising to shun Michele until she apologized. Me and Helena knew Ramona couldn't stand not talking to Michele, so we knew she would break her promise. At the end of the day, I asked Helena if maybe we took it too far but Helena said "No. She

was the one who ignored us and sat at a different table." Okay then. But not much other than that. Goodnight, diary!

February 18, 2016
Sorry I haven't written in a while. The fight with Michele has been resolved…so…yeah. I'm really busy and tired these days…so…yeah. I….The test is finally over, anyway, so now I have to wait till March to find out. Anyway, SCHOOL is stressful! I swear, people are out to get you. Anyway, I'm kind of distracted, and it's hard to focus. Anyway, tomorrow's Friday, so I'll have time to refocus. Also Michele wrote a book, and she said it had swearing and suicide in it. Okay. I'm getting tired now, so goodnight.

February 24, 2016
Dear Diary,
I read Michele's book, and it was pretty good! (No suicide). Also Helena if you're reading this, then go back and fill out the page that I wrote for you. Anyway, I got 101% on my math test, which I am really proud of. But for some reason I just feel bummed out. It's probably hormones.

Anyway, tomorrow's Thursday. And I like Thursdays. Why?
Because:

    1. Its art class at school

2. I get to prep Helena's hair for swimming, which is really pretty and never looks greasy, although even she admits she's got split ends
3. It's art class at the park!

And as always, it's getting late so goodnight!

P.S. Plus also my hair smells yummy.

February 28, 2016

Dear Diary,

Tomorrow is Leap Day! I wish their was no school. So, on Saturday, me + Helena had a sleepover at my house, and we went out for Indian food which was super spicy. When we came back, we did some spa stuff + went to bed. And I asked her whether she loved me or not, and she just kept saying "in the middle." Man, she can be so annoying sometimes! Anyway, though, we were playing on the trampoline, and she said "yes." So yay! After that, I made her say "I love you" a few times, just to be sure.

Also Ramona, if your reading this, STOP READING MY DIARY!

Oh and Mom cut my hair today. She isn't half bad at it! Anyway I'm tired. Goo…

March 3, 2016

Dear Diary,

I'm going to be honest with you. Me + Helena's relationship is pretty rocky. Helena barking orders at me and getting mad when I don't do them in time has not been fun. And no, it's not just Helena. It's also me. I've been annoying. But these days, Helena has been greedy and bossy and has been ignoring me randomly. I tried to give her the benefit of the doubt, but today was her breaking point.

She says I cheated on a Latin test (which I didn't) and says almost everything I do is annoying her, and that we aren't close friends and haven't been since 4th grade. I got really sad and started crying. I mean, I knew we weren't AS close, but I thought we were still close.

Apparently not. I cried the entire bus ride home. She unshared her Young Authors with me, so I unshared our book (The Greatest Book Ever) with her (which is probably bad, because we were working on it TOGETHER) and says from now on, she's not going to show her diary to anyone anymore, including me. Mom says she's becoming independent.

I'm really, really, really sad, and yet, only sad. Not

mad.

March 5, 2016
Dear Diary,
It's getting easier. I'm getting more and more used to the idea of a group of friends, instead of just one main friend. This feels like a breakup though, and not a friendship one. But at least we're still friends. And maybe, by the end of the year, we'll be close friends. But probably (and Helena said so herself) we will never be as close as we were in fourth grade ever again. And that's sad. But I have to move on. Clean myself up, stuff like that. We are still working on the Greatest Book Ever, and Science Olympiad together.

Anyway, enough about Helena. Today, I felt mostly and looked, well, good.
Back to Helena. Thank god me and her relationship ended up like this. What if it ended with one of us being seriously injured, or dead? THAT would be the worst. And I miss her, and I wish we could grow close again, but she believes we can't, and that it's too late. She says she doesn't love me anymore and that she hasn't for a long time.

Anyway, we went bowling today. It's getting late. Goodnight.

March 6, 2016
Dear Diary,
Me + Helena aren't as close, but we are still good friends.

Goodnight.

March 7, 2016
Dear Diary,
We made up! I think we were just making ourselves miserable, saying things like that. Helena wasn't as bad as I said she was, and I am pretty sure Helena exaggerated in her diary too. We made up in science class and went to the bathroom together. We kissed each other on the cheek, said "I love you" to each other, and pinkie-promised each other through the power of love to never fight again. This was our first,

short fight, and our last one too. We're planning on showing each other's diaries on Thursday. I hope she doesn't get too mad at what I said in the last three entries. Well, I guess we'll find out.

Also, my mom was nice enough to lend us a small table and tablecloth for science olympiad that she loves, because she TRUSTS us with it. Also when I told my mom the argument was done, she was very relieved. I'm so happy that the fight is over! It's in the past. Done. And Helena said that we can grow close again. Also, Helena's little brother Ivan got surgery today to help with health problems. Also, Helena's getting bottom braces today. Yikes! Also I learned how to do a 5-strand braid. I did it on Jessie, and it looked really cool! Now I owe her something on Wednesday. Probably a small dessert.

Anyway, Michele finished writing her book and she said that now she has nothing to live for. And I told her (in private) that she was invited to my end-of-the-year-party. Once I told her that I had a pool + trampoline and that there would be free food, her eyes completely lit up!

So now here is who I'm inviting to the party so far: Helena, Michele, Cleo. I still am undecisive about Ramona and Caroline, but their definitely a maybe. Anyway it's time to say
{Pictured: a happy crescent moon and smiling star, on the moon's hat is a pom-pom}
Goodnight!

March 12, 2016
Dear Diary,
You are almost out of paper! Anyways, yesterday Helena had a sleepover at my house to work on science olympiad, and we watched a kinda scary movie, called the Sixth Sense. It gave us the heebie-jeebies! Anyways, we <u>still</u> have to practice our script, so I have to get a good nights sleep.
Goodnight!

March 17, 2016
Dear Diary,
Me and Helena did the Science Olympiad, and we won! We got medals and shook the principal's hand and everything. I've been winning everything this year. Science Olympiad AND science fair (third place)! Also, today I realized that Helena has been getting her eyebrows waxed. I had noticed it before, I just didn't know if I was just imagining things, so I didn't say anything. Also, Ezra sent me a sincere email, saying he was trying to be nice and how he missed me. This was after he said he hated my hair and was weird. I sent him a short one back saying "It's good to hear you're back to your old self," and left. Also, I THINK (not know) that my mom is taking me + Helena to see Allegiant! I hope it's good. Also we (my fam) are invited to the Cox's this Saturday! Ugh!

Luckily, me + my mom can't stay there long because of their cat. We're allergic. And did you know Kayley secretly hates me, and Kayley + Ramona secretly hate Helena <3 ? Crazy! And I'm working on making a glitter art piece for Helena. It is a moon-crescent shape and is made out of SACRED light blue glitter. Also, we're making calendar schedules, to schedule when we will facetime + text + call each other OVER SUMMER BREAK, which might be postponed if the teachers (including my dad) do a walkout and a strike. Again.

It's getting late, so I gtg (got to go).

Goodnight!

March 24, 2016

Dear Diary,

Sorry I haven't written in a while. I just have been too tired. And the Earhart Teacher's Union IS striking, including my dad, on Friday, April 1st. So I'll go to Helena's house, where I will be doing Easter. You see, her family is really healthy, so they don't do Easter. So I am bringing Easter to her. But I'm going to put only water in one egg, so when she opens it, I'll be all like, "April Fools!" But maybe not. I don't know. Also state testing is going on right now, so BLEAH! I *think* I'm going to do it this year. I mean, I started, so might as well finish, right? Also my gymnastics competition happened, and I did mediocre. Anyway,

Goodnight!

P.S. Helena is the only person I know who can do a

GOOD sock bun.

?-?-2016

Dear Diary,
Lots of things happened. I got into Curie Academic Center and Helena got into Barton. I wish I had gotten into Barton to be with Helena, but eh, maybe its for the best. I probably would've gotten lost anyway. But my dad's trying to get me into Barton. But isn't that kind of unfair? For ME to go to Barton, without REALLY getting in? Also, my dad is pirating movies so we can watch it on the plane. It SEEMS innocent, but its actually against the law. The FBI could track him down for this. Also, I just went to Ramona's birthday party, which was "meh."
Anyway, me and Helena also did Science Olympiad at the City Competition at Barden High school. Well anyway, its getting late. So I think it's time to say
{Pictured: the most elaborate "goodnight" seen thus far}
P.S. SPRING BREAK is in a week and I'm going to Cabo San Lucas in Mexico!

June 7, 2016
Dear Diary,
I lost you! BTW, Spring Break was awesome! We went to lots of places, and I had a lot of fun. We made it

for the state Science Olympiad, got nominated for nationals, but didn't make it. My artwork made it to state, so I got a reflections award for Visual Art. Also, Michele's birthday passed. Me + Helena read her diary (I know, I know) and you know, she always complains that her life sucks all the time? She was lying! And she wrote so! Also, me + Helena finished the calendars for each other, and they look really cool! This is the end of the diary, Diary. Future Ava, hoped you liked it!

-Ava Marie Stardust

PRIMARY DOCUMENT: NOTE

{Pictured: a looseleaf piece of paper. Helena's handwriting.}

The creation of
AWESOMENESS!!!

Helena+ Ava = Awesomeness!
{Pictured underneath Helena are long eyelashes, and under Ava is "Glitta!"}

Ava I love you and you should know whatever schools we get into I promise to be your BFFAEAE forever. We will probably be separated and get really sad but there will always be forever.

{Pictured: a sweet smiley face with eyelashes}

<u>PRIMARY DOCUMENT: THE GREATEST BOOK EVER</u>

Dear Reader,
This is a book full of information for how to do stuff the RIGHT way. This book covers everything, from hair to food to organizing.
We hope you enjoy this book!

<3,
x__Ava Ochoa_____ x____Helena Pruitt_____

{Note: many of the pages were censored, the following are excerpts.}

<u>How To Put on Fancy Makeup for Girls</u>
(or guys, you do you)
1) Wash face, fix eyebrows if needed.
2) Apply foundation and blush
3) Fill in eyebrows and do eye makeup
4) Put on mascara and eyeliner
5) Fill in lips and your done!

<u>Nails</u>
Cut your nails *after* you get out of the shower. They're softer and won't fly everywhere!

<u>Giant Chocolate Covered Strawberry</u>

1) Mush up strawberries
2) Freeze as a popsicle
3) Cover in chocolate. Let harden.

{Pictured: A very hateful, targeted page, in newer handwriting, entitled: DON'T GET A BEST FRIEND! DO NOT! The rest is redacted.}

{Pictured: many empty pages}

The End
Signed,
Ava and Helena

{Pictured: a yearbook for the 6th grade graduates, class of 2016. The pages at the end were designed for student signatures. There are many "HAGS" (Have A Great Summer) and various phone numbers and emails.}

Dear Ava,

We first officially met in 4th grade where we became best friends.

We have gone through ups and downs but I hope we stay friends forever and find each other in other lives we live.

You have been an amazing friend! I'm afraid I will never find someone like you again.

We have shared many laughs (especially when I'm being dumb!) and shared tears as well.

We have been there for each other when it was needed most.

I yet again hope we will be BFFAEAE's Forever. I love you <3 !

<3,

Helena Pruitt

{ Pictured: Helena's signature, labeled "for when I'm famous")

ACKNOWLEDGEMENTS

I first want to thank Peri Multu, for always supporting my writing. My mirrorball forever and ever and ever!

Thank you to Sumiko Fujihara, the first one brave enough to read it, and for providing the beautiful cover art.

Thank you to those who finished my book, I love you and I wish I could kiss all of you on the mouth (no tongue, I keep it very tasteful).

I want to thank books, I want to thank my laptop charger, I want to thank all my friends, and everyone who gave me advice. I also want to thank everyone IN this book.

I want to thank my Catwoman barbie, my clothes folder, and my wooden hairbrush (all of which I still have). Thank you Ariana Grande for existing.

Lastly, thank you little Ava, for doing all the heavy lifting in writing this. Sorry I failed your quiz.

Ava Marie Stardust & Ava Maria Ochoa

Ava Marie Stardust is 12 years old, and she is about to start seventh grade at Curie Academic Center. She loves to write, draw, and hang out with her friends. She makes fully edited Youtube videos on her  iPad mini that have never seen the light of day, and takes herself very seriously.

Ava Maria Ochoa attends New York University's Stern School of Business, pursuing a bachelor's degree in Business in Data Science, with minors in Creative Writing and Psychology. In her free time she likes to write poetry, dance, and hang out with her friends. She also watches shows over and over until she can remember each line of dialogue in every scene, and takes herself very seriously.

Made in the USA
Las Vegas, NV
12 October 2024